MILLBURN

D0846261

C
42
PC

What Good Is an E?

by Marie Powell

amicus readers

1

Say Hello to Amicus Readers.

You'll find our helpful dog, Amicus, chasing a ball—to let you know the reading level of a book.

1

Learn to Read

Frequent repetition, high frequency words, and close photo-text matches introduce familiar topics and provide ample support for brand new readers.

2

Read Independently

Some repetition is mixed with varied sentence structures and a select amount of new vocabulary words are introduced with text and photo support.

3

Read to Know More

Interesting facts and engaging art and photos give fluent readers fun books both for reading practice and to learn about new topics.

Amicus Readers are published by Amicus
P.O. Box 1329, Mankato, MN 56002
www.amicuspublishing.us

Copyright © 2016. International copyright reserved in all countries. No part of this book may be reproduced in any form without written permission from the publisher.

Library of Congress Cataloging-in-Publication Data

Powell, Marie, 1958-
  What good is an E? / by Marie Powell.
    pages cm. -- (Vowels)
  Summary: " Beginning readers are introduced to the vowel E and its sounds and uses, including the silent E."-- Provided by publisher.
  ISBN 978-1-60753-709-0 (library binding)
  ISBN 978-1-60753-813-4 (ebook)
  1. Vowels--Juvenile literature. 2. English language--Vowels--Juvenile literature. I. Title.
  PE1157.P6934 2015
  428.1'3--dc23
                2014045765

Photo Credits: Andrey Kuzmin, cover; Shutterstock Images, 1, 3, 6, 15, 16 (top left) (bottom left) (bottom right); Polka Dot Images/Thinkstock, 5, 16 (top right); Margo Sokolovskaya/Shutterstock Images, 8; iStock/Thinkstock, 11; Jupiter Imag, BananaStock/Thinkstock, 12

Produced for Amicus by The Peterson Publishing Company and Red Line Editorial.

Editor Jenna Gleisner
Designer Craig Hinton

Printed in Malaysia
10 9 8 7 6 5 4 3 2 1

What good is an <u>E</u>? <u>E</u> is a vowel, like A, I, O, U, and Y. What sounds does <u>E</u> make?

<u>E</u> can have a long sound, like its name. <u>E</u>ve and <u>E</u>laine run a r<u>e</u>lay.

E can have a short sound. Ed and Jen will play tennis with Ted.

E can start a word. Ellen catches a butterfly and puts it in an empty jar.

E can come in the middle of a word. Ellen collects leaves to put in her jar.

E can come at the end of a word. Two Es together make a long E sound. The three of us climb the tree.

A silent E makes another vowel say its name. Shane slid down the slide. Many words use the vowel E!

Vowel: E

Which words have a long E sound?

Which words have a short E sound?

Which words have a silent E?

tennis

relay

tree

slide